THE YOUNG MONEY

FROM POCKET MONEY TO PROSPERITY

SUDHANSHU RANJAN

Copyright © Sudhanshu Ranjan
All Rights Reserved.

This book has been self-published with all reasonable efforts taken to make the material error-free by the author. No part of this book shall be used, reproduced in any manner whatsoever without written permission from the author, except in the case of brief quotations embodied in critical articles and reviews.

The Author of this book is solely responsible and liable for its content including but not limited to the views, representations, descriptions, statements, information, opinions and references ["Content"]. The Content of this book shall not constitute or be construed or deemed to reflect the opinion or expression of the Publisher or Editor. Neither the Publisher nor Editor endorse or approve the Content of this book or guarantee the reliability, accuracy or completeness of the Content published herein and do not make any representations or warranties of any kind, express or implied, including but not limited to the implied warranties of merchantability, fitness for a particular purpose. The Publisher and Editor shall not be liable whatsoever for any errors, omissions, whether such errors or omissions result from negligence, accident, or any other cause or claims for loss or damages of any kind, including without limitation, indirect or consequential loss or damage arising out of use, inability to use, or about the reliability, accuracy or sufficiency of the information contained in this book.

Made with ♥ on the Notion Press Platform
www.notionpress.com

To my family - whose quiet strength, endless patience, and unwavering belief carried me through every chapter of this journey.
Your support has been my foundation, your faith my guiding light.
This book is a reflection of your love, your sacrifice, and your silent encouragement.

With deepest gratitude,

Sudhanshu Ranjan

Contents

Foreword

In a world where money often dictates opportunities, choices, and even dreams, financial literacy is no longer a luxury—it's a life skill. And yet, most of us stumble into adulthood with little understanding of how to manage our money, let alone grow it. What if we could change that narrative early?

The Young Money: From Pocket Money to Prosperity steps into this crucial gap with simplicity, empathy, and vision. Through engaging storytelling and relatable characters, this book does what few others attempt—it brings financial wisdom to children and teens in a language they understand and enjoy.

Sudhanshu Ranjan has crafted more than just a book; he has planted a seed of financial consciousness in the fertile minds of the next generation. As a parent, teacher, or young reader, you'll find yourself smiling at the gentle lessons wrapped in everyday moments—lessons about saving, spending wisely, building discipline, and even dreaming big.

This book is timely. In an age of digital wallets and instant gratification, children need tools to pause, think, and grow a healthy relationship with money. And this book provides just that—clarity without complexity, inspiration without intimidation.

Whether you're reading this with your child or gifting it to a young dreamer, know that you are handing them more than pages—you are handing them power.

Let this book be the beginning of a journey—not just to wealth, but to wisdom.

Preface

I still remember the first time my son asked, "Papa, why can't we buy that toy today?" That innocent question sparked a conversation—not just about money, but about choices, priorities, and value. It also planted the idea for this book.

The Young Money was born out of a simple realization: our schools teach algebra, grammar, and geography—but not how to manage money. And yet, money impacts nearly every decision we make in life. Why wait until adulthood to learn financial discipline when we can start in childhood, when habits are still forming?

This book is not a textbook. It's a story—a journey through the eyes of a young boy named Vivaan and his everyday experiences. Through fun, relatable episodes, kids (and even adults) will explore practical financial lessons like saving, budgeting, goal-setting, and planning for the future. It's a blend of storytelling and financial education, carefully designed to inform, inspire, and empower.

My goal is simple: to help children become confident, conscious, and curious about money. I've intentionally used age suitable very basic financial instrument concepts, easy language, the tone warm, and the examples grounded in everyday life—so that every child, parent, and teacher can read, relate, and reflect.

If this book can spark even one meaningful money conversation in your home or classroom, it has served its purpose.

Let's raise a financially smart generation—one story at a time.

Sudhanshu Ranjan

Author

<h1 style="text-align:center">Prologue</h1>

Money—it jingles in our pockets, slips through our fingers, and powers our dreams. Yet, most of us grow up learning about it the hard way, often through mistakes that could've been avoided with a little awareness early on.

This story begins with a simple coin, a curious child, and a thoughtful parent. What starts as an innocent lesson in saving pocket money soon becomes a journey of discovery—about patience, planning, choices, and the invisible power of habits.

In this book, you will meet Vivaan, a bright 10-year-old boy with big questions and even bigger dreams. His father, Amit, becomes his first money mentor—not by giving lectures, but by engaging him in real-life decisions and small yet powerful experiments.

The Young Money is not just a financial guide. It's a tale for every child who has ever held a coin and wondered what else it could do besides buy candy. And it's for every parent who wants their child to learn the value of money—without losing the joy of childhood.

This prologue is your invitation to step into Vivaan's world. A world where money is not just counted, but understood. Not feared, but respected. And most importantly—not spent aimlessly, but used wisely.

Let's begin the journey—from pocket money to prosperity.

1

The Watch, the Wait, and the Wallet

"Look at my new watch!"

Vivaan beamed as he stretched out his arm, proudly showing off his sleek, brand-new digital watch to his friends in the playground. The black strap hugged his wrist like armour, and the shiny display blinked the time with every little movement he made. It wasn't just a watch — to Vivaan, it was a badge of pride.

Just wait till Rohit sees this! He thought, trying to act casual, even though excitement bubbled inside him.

Only yesterday, Rohit had strutted around with his flashy new smart watch, showing off features Vivaan didn't even understand. Rohit had teased everyone, saying, "You guys are living in the past! Look at what the future looks like!"

Well, now the future had arrived on Vivaan's wrist.

"Whoa, cool watch!" someone said. "Can it show steps?"

Vivaan shrugged dramatically. "Of course it can. And the date. And alarms. And a light too!"

The kids surrounded him in admiration, and Vivaan soaked in every bit of it. His moment had arrived.

Meanwhile, back at home, his father Amit had just walked through the door after a long, exhausting day at work. His shoulders drooped as he placed his bag on the table.

"Where's Vivaan?" he asked, loosening his tie.

Neetu smiled knowingly as she handed him a steaming cup of tea. "Where else? He dashed off to the playground the moment he got home — showing off his new prized possession."

Amit took the cup and sighed. "That boy... his demands are growing every day. A new cricket bat last month, those expensive sneakers, and now this watch. If we don't step in now, he'll think money grows on trees."

Neetu nodded thoughtfully. "I agree. We need to teach him what goes behind the things he enjoys."

Amit sipped his tea slowly, a quiet determination settling on his face. "Yes. It's time he learns the value of money — not just its price." He told Neetu that he is going out and let Vivaan know he is in office still. Neetu was surprised and before she could ask the reason, Amit fled out.

That evening, Vivaan burst into the house, his stomach growling after all the running around.

"Mom! I'm starving! What's for dinner?" he called out, kicking off his shoes at the door.

"Dinner's ready. Go wash your hands," Neetu said, setting plates on the table.

Vivaan plopped down at the table, rubbing his hands together eagerly. But he frowned as he looked around. "Where's Dad?"

"He's still at work," Neetu replied.

Vivaan blinked. "Still? But it's so late!"

"He's working late — for us," Neetu said softly.

Vivaan tilted his head, confused. "For us? But... shouldn't he be here *with* us then?"

Neetu sat beside him, her tone gentle. "Why do you think Dad goes to work?"

Vivaan looked puzzled. "To... earn money?"

"Yes. But do you know how much time, effort, and sacrifice that takes?" she asked, brushing a lock of hair from his forehead.

Vivaan looked down at his plate, suddenly not feeling so hungry. "I miss him."

"I know. But sometimes, to give us the life we enjoy, he has to give up time with us. That's what makes his love so powerful."

Vivaan was quiet after that. He ate slowly and went to bed without protest. The shiny watch on his wrist no longer felt quite so magical.

The next morning, he jumped out of bed and ran to the living room. He found his father fast asleep on the couch, still in his work clothes. Neetu placed a finger on her lips. "Shhh... he got home very late. Let him rest."

Vivaan tiptoed closer, wanting to hug him, but instead just watched his father sleep, tired and peaceful. Something tugged at his heart.

He dressed quietly and left for school.

Once Vivaan was out the door, Neetu turned to Amit. "Okay, tell me. What's this all about? Coming home late, looking exhausted — what are you trying to do?"

Amit gave a tired smile. "Patience. A lesson learned through experience stays longer than a lecture. I'm planting seeds."

For three more days, the same routine continued. Amit came home late. Vivaan saw him only for a few minutes each morning. And with every passing day, the sparkle in Vivaan's eyes dimmed just a little.

By Friday night, Vivaan sat quietly in his room. He stared at his watch, but now it didn't bring him the same joy. It just reminded him of how little he'd seen his father lately.

I didn't want *this*, he thought.

Then came Saturday morning.

Vivaan woke up hoping it would be different. To his delight, Amit was already at the breakfast table.

"Get ready, champ," he said with a smile. "We're heading out."

Vivaan's eyes lit up. "Where?"

"You'll see."

The two of them set off to the nearby vegetable market. Amit handed Vivaan a small pouch with some cash inside. "You're in charge of this," he said. "As I pick out things, I'll ask for money. Keep track of it."

Vivaan puffed out his chest, feeling important.

As they walked through the market, Amit selected vegetables and asked for small amounts — ₹40 here, ₹90 there. Vivaan handed over the money each time, trying his best to remember the amounts. But with the noise and excitement, he soon lost track.

Once they returned home, Amit sat him down. "Alright, tell me — how much money did we spend today?"

Vivaan's face froze. "Umm... I don't know. I wasn't keeping count."

Amit pretended to look surprised. "Oh no! I forgot to count how much I gave you. How will we figure it out now?"

Vivaan frowned. "Wait! If we add up the prices of the vegetables, we'll know how much we spent!"

Amit grinned. "Exactly. Let's do it."

Together, they listed every item and calculated the total — ₹550.

"See?" Amit said. "Money isn't just about spending. It's about knowing where every rupee goes."

Vivaan looked thoughtful. "It's not as easy as it looks."

Amit smiled. "But it becomes easier when you pay attention."

Just then, Neetu joined them. "Vivaan, we want you to start managing small purchases. But first, make a list of the things you want and how often you need them. We'll decide how much pocket money to give you."

The word "pocket money" echoed in Vivaan's ears like magic. His eyes widened. He froze like a statue, then suddenly darted into his room.

Neetu laughed. "Where's he going now?"

Amit chuckled. "To plan his new empire."

Sure enough, Vivaan came back with a notebook, his pen already scribbling furiously. "Snacks... Comics... Extra pens... Hmm... maybe a new football too..."

Amit leaned back, watching his son with pride. The journey had begun — one rupee at a time.

2
The Wish List

Vivaan sat cross-legged on the floor, eyes sparkling, notebook in hand, scribbling furiously like a mad scientist. "Chocolates, pencils, a fancy eraser, a Spiderman water bottle, a digital lunchbox, football shoes, superhero socks, winter gloves—wait, do I need gloves? Doesn't matter—gloves, a pencil box with a secret code lock... Oh, and bubble gum. Lots of it!"

Amit watched from across the room, eyebrows slowly climbing his forehead.
He leaned in, pretending to squint. "Vivaan... are you planning to open a stationery shop?"

Vivaan giggled. "No, Dad! This is my wish list—for when I start getting pocket money!"

Amit raised the paper gently like it was a legal contract. "Hmm... a *Spiderman* bottle? But your bottle works just fine. And gloves? Are you planning a trip to Antarctica?"

Vivaan's grin began to fade. He had imagined freedom—a life where he could buy whatever he wanted, no questions asked. But now... there were questions.

Amit noticed the flicker of disappointment in his son's eyes. He patted the floor next to him.
"Come here, champ."

Vivaan slid over, and Amit gently pulled him onto his lap.

"You know," he began, "it's completely okay to want nice things. But let me tell you a little secret—sometimes, we want things not because we need them, but because someone else has them."

Vivaan looked puzzled.

Amit smiled. "Who has that cool water bottle you mentioned?"

"Tushar," Vivaan replied instantly. "It has Spiderman swinging through fire!"

Amit chuckled. "It *is* cool. But what if next week Tushar gets a new one with Spiderman and Iron Man? Will you want that one too?"

Vivaan paused. "Maybe..."

"And the week after that, maybe he gets one with a built-in torch."

Vivaan's eyebrows shot up. "Wait, those exist?!"

Amit laughed. "Exactly. That's how it goes. There will always be something newer, flashier, and cooler. But chasing after every new thing can drain your money faster than you think."

Vivaan nodded slowly, the gears in his head beginning to turn.

"Come," Amit said, standing up. "Let's make a quick trip to Das Babu's shop. Mom needs a few things."

As they stepped outside, Amit pointed to their modest white sedan. "Do you like our car?"

Vivaan nodded. "Of course! It's super comfy!"

Amit pointed to the gleaming BMW parked next door. "What about that one?"

Vivaan squinted. "It's nice... but it's blue. I like our car better."

Amit smiled. "See? Just because something is more expensive doesn't always mean it's better for *us*."

Vivaan tilted his head, thinking. The lesson was subtle, but it made sense.

At Das Babu's shop, Amit picked up some groceries and household items. Then he turned to Vivaan. "Alright, champ. Your turn. You can choose one item for yourself. Anything you *need*."

Vivaan's eyes scanned the shelves—glitter pens, superhero pencils, shiny erasers calling out like sirens. His hand moved toward the flashiest pencil box, but then he paused.

He turned to Amit. "Actually... I think I just need a sharpener. Mine's broken."

Amit's heart swelled. "Now that's a wise choice, buddy."

On their walk home, Vivaan looked up thoughtfully. "Dad... do you ever want to buy silly things too?"

Amit laughed. "All the time! Just last week, I saw a smart toaster that talks."

Vivaan's jaw dropped. "Seriously?"

"But then I asked myself—do I *need* a talking toaster, or do I just want it because it sounds cool?"

Vivaan giggled. "You definitely don't need a talking toaster."

"Exactly," Amit said with a wink. "That's what I want you to start doing too."

Back home, Amit handed Vivaan the notebook again.

"Take another look at your wish list. Think it through. What's a *need*, and what's just a *want*?"

Vivaan nodded, flipping to a fresh page and scribbling with more intention this time. Chocolates? Keep. Fancy pencil box? Maybe not. Football shoes? Yes, he needed new ones for school.

When he was done, Amit glanced at the list and quickly totalled it in his head.   ₹480.

"Okay, here's the deal," Amit announced. "You'll get   ₹500 as pocket money every month."

Vivaan jumped up, fists in the air. "YES!"

"—but," Amit added, raising a finger, "you must tell me before buying anything over   ₹100 or anything not on your list."

Vivaan nodded eagerly. "Deal!"

Then, Amit's tone shifted slightly, more serious but kind.

"One more thing—it's exam season. Let's start this new journey from April, okay? That gives you time to prepare *and* plan."

Vivaan gave a thoughtful nod. "Okay, Dad. April it is."

As he headed to his room, Vivaan looked back with a grin. He wasn't just getting money. He was getting something far cooler—the power to choose.

3

The First Pay Day and The Empty Envelope

It was the 1ˢᵗ of April—April fool's Day. But Vivaan wasn't worried. His father might love a good joke, but not about *this*. Today was the day. *The Pocket Money Day*.

Vivaan had been counting down to this morning like it was his birthday. As he got dressed for school, he couldn't stop glancing at his father, waiting—*hoping*—for a sign. But Amit said nothing. He calmly buttered his toast and sipped his chai like it was any other Tuesday.

Just when Vivaan thought he might explode with anticipation, Amit finally said with a smile, "Son, I've kept your pocket money in an envelope inside your drawer."

Vivaan's eyes lit up. "Really?!"

Without another word, he zoomed into his room, flung open the drawer, and found the brown envelope waiting like treasure. He opened it carefully and counted the crisp ₹100/50/20 and 10 notes. Once. Twice. Just to be sure.

₹500. His first ever. *His own.*

Grinning ear to ear, he tucked the envelope into his school bag. But as he zipped it up, Amit appeared at the door and said gently, "Vivaan, it's smarter to carry only a small amount with you. Not the whole ₹500."

Vivaan blinked. "But it's my money! Can't I take it all?"

"Of course," said Amit, "but let me ask—are you going to spend all of it today?"

Vivaan shook his head slowly.

"So if you carry just ₹20 or ₹30 and keep the rest safe, you lower the risk of losing it. Makes sense?"

Vivaan paused... and nodded. He took out ₹20 and slipped it into his pocket. It felt light—but powerful. That day at school, Vivaan spent all ₹20. Chocolates for himself and his friends. A sticker sheet from the school canteen. He was on top of the world. *Pocket money was freedom.*

In the days that followed, his spending spree continued. ₹40 on a fancy ruler. ₹30 on a cartoon keychain. ₹50 for mini treats. A few rupees here, a few there. Each small decision felt harmless... until, one morning, he opened his envelope and found it empty. It was only the 20th of April.

Vivaan stared at the empty envelope in disbelief. Had he been robbed? Did he miscalculate? Or... had he really spent it all?

Panicking, he went back through his mental notes. One by one, he remembered the small "harmless" purchases. They had added up like invisible raindrops until the storm arrived.

"I need more money," he muttered to himself.

So Vivaan sat down with his notebook again. This time, he made a new budget. A *serious* one. He listed stationery, cricket ball, snacks, and a glow-in-the-dark ruler (again). This time, the total came to ₹700.

He practiced how he'd pitch it. He rehearsed his serious face in the mirror. That evening, armed with his "revised budget," Vivaan approached his dad in the living room.

Amit looked up from his newspaper and smiled. "Yes, CEO Vivaan?"

Vivaan took a deep breath. "Dad, I think we need to revise our agreement. ₹500 isn't enough. I made a new budget—it comes to ₹700."

Intrigued, Amit set the newspaper aside. He examined the neat list. Snacks. Keychain. Glow ruler. Pens. Chocolates.

"Hmm," he said, "This is quite detailed. But tell me something—how many of these are *needs*, and how many are *wants*?"

Vivaan froze. That ruler again. The keychain. Maybe... they weren't really "needs."

Amit continued, "You see, spending is easy. But managing money—that's where the real skill lies. If I increase your allowance now, you might still finish it early again. That won't solve the problem."

Vivaan lowered his head. "But I didn't waste it. I just didn't plan well..."

"Exactly," said Amit, placing a hand on his son's shoulder. "This isn't about being wrong—it's about learning. Come on, let me show you something."

They walked to the study, where Amit pulled out a whiteboard. With a marker, he drew three columns and wrote:

Vivaan's Pocket Money Plan

Needs | Wants | Savings

Vivaan tilted his head. "Savings? Why savings? Isn't pocket money for spending?"

"That's what most people think," Said Amit, "but even a little saving can go a long way."

He pointed to the board.

"Needs are essentials—things you must have. Wants are fun but not necessary. And savings? That's your future fund. Want to buy a football? Or maybe something big someday? This is how you do it."

He scribbled under the columns:

- Needs – ₹200
- Wants – ₹200
- Savings – ₹100
  Total: ₹500

"This way," Amit explained, "you have money for what you need, some for fun, and some for the future. It's not about more money—it's about smarter money."

Vivaan's eyes sparkled with understanding. "So I'm like... the boss of my money?"

Amit laughed. "Exactly! You're the CEO of Vivaan Enterprises. And your first job as CEO is to make your money last."

Vivaan saluted. "Yes, sir! From tomorrow, my company is under budget control!"

They both laughed, and Amit knew—the lesson had landed.

4

The CEO's First Test

The next morning, Vivaan bounced out of bed with a spark in his eyes. He stood before the mirror, straightened his shoulders like a young executive, and grinned.

"Vivaan Enterprises is now officially operational!" he declared to his reflection.

He pulled out his envelope of pocket money and, just like Dad had taught him, sorted it into three labelled pouches: Needs, Wants, and Savings. It felt like setting up a real business.

But being a CEO wasn't going to be easy.

At school that very day, temptation arrived wearing neon colours. Arjun, his best friend, had a set of highlighters that glowed like lightsabers.

"You can get them for just sixty rupees at the bookstore," Arjun whispered. "They're amazing!"

Vivaan's fingers twitched toward his backpack. He knew his Wants pouch had two hundred rupees. Sixty wasn't a big deal—except it was only the beginning of the month. If he spent it now, he'd have to be extra careful later.

He stared at the highlighters for a moment, then imagined himself sitting at a CEO's desk, making decisions not just for today—but for the future.

"Maybe next month," he told Arjun with a small smile. "Right now, I've got a budget to stick to."

Arjun blinked. "You sound like a grown-up."

"Not a grown-up," Vivaan said with a proud little grin. "Just a CEO."

That evening, he shared the story with Amit, who clapped him on the back.

"You didn't say no to the highlighters—you just said not right now. That's discipline, son. And that's your first real step into financial wisdom."

Vivaan glowed. He hadn't just saved money—he'd made a choice. Vivaan Enterprises was off to a solid start.

But he had no idea that the real tests were just around the corner.

A few days later, a wave of excitement spread through the school corridors. Posters went up. Announcements buzzed through the loudspeakers.

The book fair had arrived.

For students, it was no less than a festival. Storybooks, puzzles, fancy pens, superhero diaries—it was a wonderland of colors and curiosity. When the day finally came, Vivaan rushed into the hall, eyes wide, heart thumping.

And then he saw it.

A limited-edition Brain Booster Puzzle Set. It had flashing lights and timer counters and claimed to improve memory. For Vivaan, who loved a challenge, it was love at first sight.

The price tag read   ₹120.

He quickly unzipped his Wants pouch.   ₹140 remained. Buying the puzzle would leave him with just   ₹ 20—and it was only the 10th of the month.

"It's educational," he reasoned. "It boosts memory. That's sort of a need... right?"

He stood frozen, torn between logic and longing. His eyes drifted toward his Savings pouch. He could dip in—just this once. No one would know.

And then, somewhere deep inside, a voice echoed. His father's voice.

"It's not about denying yourself. It's about knowing when to say yes... and when to wait."

Vivaan closed his eyes for a second. Then, instead of rushing to the counter, he pulled out his notebook. He wrote down the name of the puzzle, its price, and the stall number. And then, with one last glance, he walked away.

That evening, he told Amit everything.

"I didn't buy it. But I really, really wanted to."

Amit looked at him with a mix of curiosity and pride. "So what did the CEO of Vivaan Enterprises decide?"

"We're saving up for it. Maybe next month. Or maybe I'll find something even better."

Amit smiled. "That's what vision looks like. You're not just spending anymore. You're strategizing."

Vivaan nodded. It felt good to walk away with his head held high.

The next morning, he sat at his study table with sketch pens, a ruler, and a mission. With care and precision, he created a colourful chart titled:

Vivaan Enterprises: Savings Goal Tracker

🎯 Goal: Brain Booster Puzzle Set – ₹120

He drew four boxes, each representing   ₹30. Every time he saved that amount, he would color one in.

When Amit peeked in, Vivaan proudly pointed to his chart.

"We're tracking investments now, Dad. Vivaan Enterprises doesn't just save—we plan."

Amit chuckled. "A CEO with vision and design skills. What a combo."

Over the next few days, Vivaan stuck to his plan. He skipped a candy sale. Ignored the call of impulse. Every ₹ 30 saved felt like another brick in his castle.

One lazy afternoon, he was sprawled on the floor, crayons scattered around him. He was drawing a football match between "Vivaan XI" and "The Monsters." In one corner of the page, he drew a little treasure chest labelled "Puzzle Fund."

Amit passed by and laughed.

"What's that chest for? Hiding chocolate?"

"Nooo," Vivaan said with mock seriousness. "It's for my imaginary savings. I color it every time I add ₹30 to the puzzle fund."

Amit smiled. "Want me to show you how some people make real savings charts?"

"Like pirates?"

"Sort of," Amit said with a grin. "But instead of gold coins, we use pocket money."

They sat down and built a simple chart using graph paper. Amit guided Vivaan gently, letting him discover the joy of reaching small milestones.

"Grown-ups use this method too," Amit said. "For saving up for big things—cars, trips, even homes."

Vivaan beamed. "Vivaan Enterprises is levelling up."

But just as he found his rhythm, life threw a curveball.

The landline rang. It was Karan, his classmate.

"Hey, Vivaan, I am short by ₹50 for my Football tournament trip fee, can you lend me? I'll return it next month."

Vivaan looked at his pouches. That was nearly half a block on his puzzle chart. He covered the receiver and turned to Amit.

"What if he forgets to return it?" he asked.

"How would that make you feel?"

"Angry... and a little sad."

"And if he does return it?"

"I'll feel good. But I'll still be nervous till then."

Amit nodded. "So maybe there's a middle ground. Help your friend, but protect your treasure chest too."

Vivaan returned to the phone. "Karan, I can give you ₹20 today. Maybe you can ask someone else for the rest?"

It wasn't perfect. But it felt right.

That night, Vivaan told his mother he was now budgeting like Dad—just with more drawings and snacks.

She burst out laughing. "Sounds like Vivaan Enterprises is in very good hands."

Then came another surprise.

The school announced a "Fun Day" with games, no uniforms, and a pop-up tuck shop. Posters flew through the class. Kids were buzzing with excitement.

"Did you see those laser key chains?"

"I'm getting the glitter cap!"

Vivaan's eyes lit up when he saw a flyer in someone's hand.

A Talking Calculator.   ₹250.

It could do math. It told jokes. It lit up and made robot sounds. It was everything a kid could dream of.

That evening, without updating his chart, Vivaan quietly emptied his Savings pouch. He even took out ₹50 from his Wants.

"I'll rebuild next month," he whispered.

He didn't tell Amit.

The next day at the carnival, he handed over the money and bought the calculator. For the first ten minutes, it was amazing.

Then a button jammed. And all it would say was: "Seven! Seven! Seven!"

His friends laughed and lost interest. By the time Vivaan reached home, he was staring at his treasure chest drawing with a lump in his throat.

He had colored in three blocks. Now it felt like he'd erased them all.

Amit noticed his silence.

"Something on your mind, CEO?"

Vivaan nodded slowly. "I spent my savings. On a talking calculator. But now it's stuck on... seven."

Amit tried not to laugh. "Sounds like your calculator has opinions."

Vivaan didn't laugh. He looked down.

"I wish I waited. Like I did with the puzzle."

Amit sat beside him. "That's how experience feels. You made a choice, you learned from it. Now Vivaan Enterprises is not just saving—it's growing."

Vivaan gave a small smile. "So... can I reset my chart and start again?"

Amit stood and saluted.

"Reset the board, Commander Vivaan. This month wasn't perfect—but the next one belongs to you."

5

Vivaan Enterprises Goes Banking

Lesson: Importance of Side Hustles, Emergency Funds, and Saving in a Bank.

The first day of June brought a fresh breeze—and a fresh mind set. Vivaan stood proudly before his cupboard, where a brand-new chart was pinned up like a company notice. It read:

💼 **Vivaan Enterprises – June Ledger**
Savings Goal: Brain Booster Puzzle Set (Still!) – ₹120
Current Balance: ₹0
Status: *Reboot Mode Activated*
New Section: ↻ *Plan B Fund – For Surprises & Silly Mistakes*

Amit, catching sight of the chart as he sipped his morning tea, raised an eyebrow and smiled.

"What's this Plan B Fund, Mr CEO?"

Vivaan, chewing thoughtfully on the end of his pencil, replied, "It's for emergencies... like if I suddenly fall in love with another 'talking calculator.'" Amit laughed. "Smart move. Even real companies keep emergency funds. You're thinking like a pro."

Later that week, while helping his mom water the balcony plants, Vivaan was still humming a tune when Amit strolled over and said casually, "You know... when I was your age, I used to help my uncle wash his scooter or organize his books. He'd pay me a small bonus." Vivaan's eyes lit up.

"Wait... I could do stuff like that too? Like, earn extra money?" Amit gave a nonchalant shrug. "Well, Vivaan Enterprises could start offering services—book organizing, garden help, maybe even babysitting your cousin during cartoons. You'd just need your first client..." He nodded toward Neetu, who was watching from the kitchen window with a smirk.

Vivaan turned dramatically. "Maaa... any jobs available? Vivaan Enterprises is expanding operations!" Neetu grinned. "Actually, I do need someone to fold the laundry every weekend. If you do it neatly, I'll pay ₹20 per week." Vivaan gave a mock salute. "Deal! Vivaan Enterprises is now Vivaan Enterprises Pvt. Ltd. — with side hustles!"

Over the next few weeks, things were looking up. Vivaan stuck to his goals. From pocket money and chores, he managed to save ₹500. Another ₹60 came from folding laundry and watering the plants. And ₹40—carefully tucked into a reused jam jar—went straight into the Plan B Fund, safely labelled:

"In case of silly spending."

One Sunday morning, Vivaan sat at the dining table, surrounded by his wealth. Coins, tens, twenties—all neatly sorted into piles next to a tall glass of mango milkshake. He was humming with satisfaction. Amit, reading the newspaper nearby, peeked over his glasses.

"Whoa! Looks like Vivaan Enterprises is running out of vault space." Vivaan beamed. "Yup! ₹600 and counting. I'm so close to the puzzle now. Plus ₹40 in the Plan B jar!" Amit leaned back thoughtfully. "That's impressive.

But what if someone knocks over your drawer and the coins fall behind the cupboard? Or worse... what if our pet pug Patty, thinks your Plan B jar is a new chew toy?" Vivaan's eyes widened in horror.

"Nooo! That's my money!"

Amit smiled. "Exactly. That's why people use banks. They're like superhero vaults—safe, secure, and even better, your money grows there."

"Grows? Like magic?" Vivaan asked, now on the edge of his chair. "Not magic—interest," Amit said, grinning.

"It's the bank's way of thanking you for keeping your money with them." Vivaan blinked. "Wait... they pay me to keep my money safe?"

"Exactly. And they help you keep track of it too. No more lost coins under the bed." Vivaan's voice turned hopeful. "Can I open a real account? Like, for kids?" Amit sipped his tea. "You actually can. It's called a 'Junior Account.'

We'll go tomorrow and ask." Vivaan stood up and bowed dramatically. "CEO Vivaan is ready to go Banking!"

The next morning, Vivaan wore his "official" company tee—a regular white shirt with a hand-drawn treasure chest and a big dollar sign. As they stepped into the bank, Vivaan looked around wide-eyed. The tall counters, typing sounds, and soft background music made it feel like a treasure cave for grown-ups.

"It's like a gold vault!" he whispered. Amit chuckled. "No gold floors to walk on, but you're close." They were greeted by a friendly officer, Ms Palak. "Good morning! How can I help you?"

Amit smiled. "We'd like to open a Junior Account for my son." Vivaan stood tall. "I know what a bank account is. It's like a treasure chest. You store your money safely, and it grows with something called... interest!"

Ms Palak laughed. "That's exactly right! And today, you'll get your very own passbook and card." She handed him a shiny green passbook with his name on it. "Each time you add or take out money, it gets recorded here. And here's your debit card—you can use it to withdraw money when needed." Vivaan stared at it like it was a magical key from a Tenali Raman story.

"This is real?" "Very real," said Amit. "But use it wisely. Save first. Spend later." Ms Palak added, "Every deposit is like planting a seed. The more you water it—with savings—the bigger your tree grows."

Vivaan's face lit up. "I'm going to grow a giant savings tree!"

On the way home, Vivaan couldn't stop talking. "I'm going to save every rupee now. No more silly toys. Vivaan Enterprises is officially banking!" Back in his room, he pulled out his notebook and began designing a new chart with colored pens:

🌱 **Vivaan Enterprises Growth Plan**
• Goal: Brain Booster Puzzle – ₹120
• Plan B Fund: ₹50
• Savings Tree: 🏦 (New Bank Account!)
• Next Deposit: ₹100 – Coming Soon!

Amit peeked into the room, quietly watching his son plan his finances like a seasoned CFO. And though the Brain Booster Puzzle still hadn't arrived, Amit knew something far more valuable had begun to take shape—the roots of discipline, responsibility, and a lifelong journey toward prosperity.

6

Vivaan Enterprises Goes Public

By September, Vivaan's savings had started to look impressive.

Every month, he deposited ₹300–₹400 from his pocket money into his new junior account. He continued helping around the house—folding clothes, watering plants, and tidying up—for small bonuses his mom quietly slipped into his piggy bank.

Gone were the impulsive buys. No more random toys or frequent treats. Every purchase was planned and logged in his notebook, beneath a personal mantra he had penned:

Vivaan Enterprises Rule:

Never spend just because you can. Spend when it really counts.

By the end of the month, he had ₹2,200 in his bank account and ₹200 in his Plan B jar.

One Saturday morning, Amit seemed unusually quiet at breakfast. His tea sat untouched. Vivaan noticed.

"Dad… you okay?"

Amit gave a faint smile. "Just some unexpected expenses. The car needed repairs, and Nana and Mama haven't been well. I had to send money for their treatment. Things will be tight for the next two months."

Vivaan nodded slowly. He didn't fully understand, but he knew it was serious.

A few days later, October 1st came and went—no mention of pocket money.

Vivaan didn't bring it up either.

That evening, he opened his notebook to a fresh page:

October Budget: No New Pocket Money Month
• Available Balance: ₹2,400
• Needs-Only Spending Rule: Activated
• Goal: No spending unless absolutely necessary
• Emergency Mood: 💡 Stay Sharp, Stay Steady

In the weeks that followed, Vivaan adjusted effortlessly.

He fixed his old pencil box with tape. Reused a nearly new notebook. Skipped the fancy eraser he'd wanted.

When his shoelace snapped at school, he asked Neetu to stitch it and wore his backup sneakers for a week.

He started packing extra snacks from home instead of buying anything from the school canteen.

Amit noticed—all of it.

One evening, he asked, "Vivaan, how have you been managing without your pocket money?"

Vivaan looked up from his notebook and smiled.

"I'm okay, Dad. I used a little from my Plan B fund and some from my bank account. I didn't buy anything fun, but I have everything I need."

Amit was stunned—and deeply moved.

He reached across the table, gently holding Vivaan's hand.

"You've done something most adults struggle to do. You understood priorities. I'm so, so proud of you."

Vivaan grinned. "Vivaan Enterprises runs on smart planning now, Dad."

Amit laughed. "Clearly. You just gave me a bit of financial advice without even knowing it."

That Sunday, Amit surprised Vivaan with a handmade certificate:

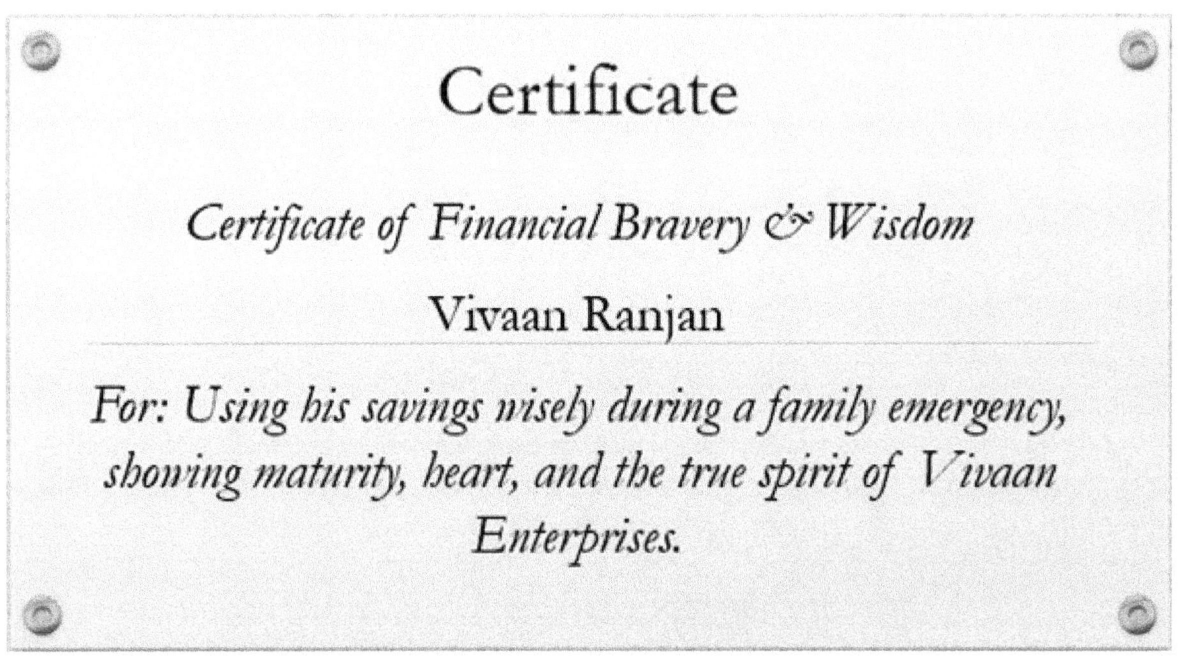

Vivaan taped it proudly on his cupboard, right above his savings chart.
That night, as he slid   ₹50 back into his Plan B jar, he whispered,
"Not just for me. For the family too."

Vivaan Enterprises Goes Public

In the last week of September, Vivaan's school announced a special event:
"My World, My Way" – A Show & Tell Celebration of Passions and Hobbies.
Students were invited to present something they had created or learned over the past year.
That evening at dinner, Vivaan lit up.
"Dad, I want to talk about Vivaan Enterprises! Can I?"
Amit paused mid-bite, then smiled. "I was hoping you'd say that."
Vivaan got to work. He gathered his savings charts, his first envelope of pocket money, the Plan B jar, his mini ledger, and of course, the certificate.
He even drew a logo: a piggy bank wearing sunglasses, crossed by a pencil and ruler.

Amit helped him design a simple presentation board. They titled it:

🏛 Vivaan Enterprises: How I Learned to Be the Boss of My Money
Mission: Save Smart. Spend Wise. Help Family When Needed.
Founder & CEO: Vivaan
Established: April 1st (but no, it's not a prank!)

On the big day, Vivaan wore his neatest uniform and pinned a badge: **Junior Money Boss.**
His table displayed colourful charts, his passbook, the "Plan B Fund" jar, and a bold sign:
"Money is not just for spending—it's for thinking!"
When his turn came, Vivaan stood tall and began:
"Hi, I'm Vivaan. I started Vivaan Enterprises with my first pocket money in April. At first, I wanted to buy everything—fancy erasers, Spiderman bottles, even a pencil box with a secret code..."
Laughter echoed.
"But then, my dad taught me how to make a list, plan a budget, and save for emergencies. I even opened a real bank account!"
Vivaan explained his strategies – Needs | Wants | Savings
Silence fell. Eyes widened.
"Last month, my dad couldn't give me pocket money. There was a family emergency. But I used my savings only for needs—and I didn't ask for more. That's when I realised—money isn't just about buying. It's about being ready."
Applause burst across the room—first from his teacher, then the parents, then the whole hall.
Amit, standing at the back, clapped the loudest.

After the event, Vivaan's teacher approached Amit.

"Mr Amit, I think Vivaan Enterprises should visit every classroom next month. We're planning a Financial Awareness Week for kids. Would you and Vivaan lead a session?"

Amit looked at his son.

Vivaan's eyes sparkled.

"We'd love to!" he said without hesitation.

That night, as Amit tucked him into bed, Vivaan whispered,

"Dad... this has been the best month of my life."

Amit smiled, "That's because you're not just earning money, Vivaan. You're earning wisdom."

Vivaan yawned and smiled sleepily,

"And one day, Vivaan Enterprises will open branches... everywhere."

7

Vivaan Enterprises Presents: Financial Awareness Week!

The next few weeks were a whirlwind for Vivaan. After his big moment at the Show & Tell event, Mrs Sharma invited Amit and Vivaan to co-lead **Financial Awareness Week**—a five-day school-wide event to help kids become smarter with money.

Amit smiled when he heard the news. "Looks like Vivaan Enterprises is expanding!"

Vivaan grinned. "Time to mentor some junior branches."

Show and Tell – My Money Story

Vivaan walked into school wearing his "Junior Money Boss" badge and carrying his ledger, savings chart, Plan B jar, and the now-famous **Certificate of Financial Bravery**. His table had a big title board:

Vivaan Enterprises

Mission: Save Smart. Spend Wise. Help Others When You Can.

One by one, he told the story of his first pocket money, how he used to make impulse purchases, and how he'd learned to plan better.

Students were intrigued. They asked questions:

"How much do you save each month?"

"Did you ever regret spending on something silly?"

"How do you say no to snacks?"

Vivaan answered like a seasoned speaker, pausing before the final message:

"It's not about how much money you have. It's about how much you **think** before using it."

Budget the Birthday Party

Amit joined for with a challenge game:

Budget the Birthday Party!

Kids were given   ₹500 in play money and had to plan a party—cake, balloons, snacks, games, and return gifts—all within budget.

Some spent   ₹300 on a giant cake and couldn't afford return gifts. Others skipped food to buy fancy decorations.

Vivaan floated between teams, gently nudging them:

"Do you need both samosas *and* cupcakes?"

"Could you make return gifts instead of buying?"

By the end, students were surprised at how hard budgeting really was—but also how **fun** it could be.

Saving for the Future – Plan B Power

Vivaan led this with a jar in his hand.

"This is my Plan B Jar. It helped me during a tough month when Dad couldn't give pocket money."

He told the story of the emergency—how he didn't complain, reused things, and still managed without buying new stuff.

Heads nodded, including the teachers'.

Later that day, during lunch break near the swings, Vivaan's friend Aryan approached him, hands deep in his pockets.

"Vivaan... I messed up. I spent all my pocket money on candy and action figures. Now Mom wants me to buy a gift for my cousin's birthday, but I have nothing left."

Vivaan leaned back thoughtfully. "That's tough. But let me ask—did you **need** what you bought?"

Aryan sighed. "No. I just... wanted them. They were on sale."

Vivaan gave a gentle smile. "We've all been there. But here's the deal: you can't undo it, but you *can* be smart now. Why not buy something small but thoughtful? Maybe even make something."

Aryan's eyes lit up. "I could draw a superhero card! And buy a chocolate bar. That'll be enough, right?"
Vivaan nodded. "Perfect. That's called **smart spending after a mistake.**"

Junior Money Clubs Begin!

Students from all grades began forming little groups to track their savings and make "Plan B jars." Mrs Sharma announced that the school would start a **Junior Money Club** officially next term—and it would be led by none other than **Vivaan and Mr Amit.**

Each class had to pick a money-related project—reusing notebooks, pooling pocket money for charity, or running a mini thrift exchange.

Aryan came running up to Vivaan with a handmade badge:
"Look! Vivaan Enterprises – Junior Branch, Aryan Nagar!"
Vivaan burst out laughing. "We're going global already!"

Celebration & Wisdom Sharing

At the closing assembly, the principal called Vivaan to the stage:
"This week, one student didn't just teach us about money—he showed us leadership, empathy, and wisdom beyond his years."

Vivaan blushed as the school handed him a new certificate:

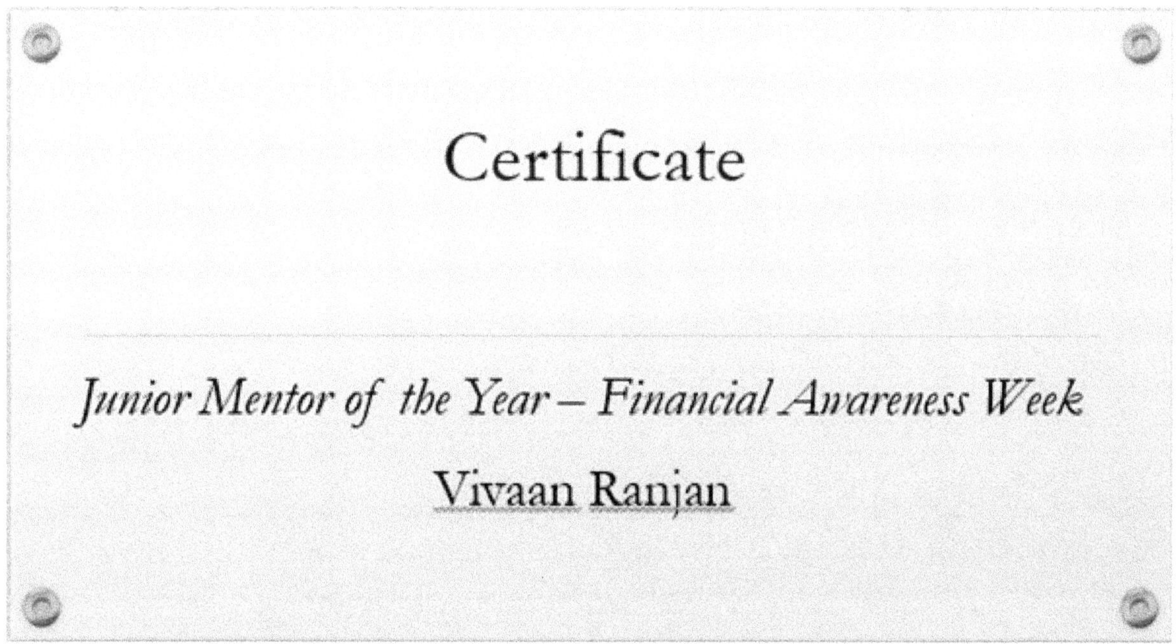

Then Mrs Sharma turned to the class. "Vivaan, would you like to share one final tip?"

Vivaan stepped forward, nervous but proud.

"If you plan well, keeping in mind your needs, wants & savings before you spend it, you will certainly make a better decision. In the long run this habit will be tremendously fruitful."

The room fell quiet. Then came a long, heartfelt applause.

That night, as Vivaan slipped into bed, he whispered,

"Dad... Aryan says he wants to be CEO of his own money too."

Amit chuckled. "Looks like you've started a financial revolution."

Vivaan smiled, eyes half-closed.

"Vivaan Enterprises... Now hiring wisdom."

8

Vivaan Enterprises: The Money That Grows on Its Own

Vivaan was now 12 years old.

Two years had passed since his first pocket money, and Vivaan Enterprises was no longer just a little project. It had grown into a full-fledged routine—his little notebook ledger had turned into an Excel sheet (which Amit proudly helped set up), his savings had crossed a few thousand rupees, and he now managed his own digital piggy bank app to track expenses.

One Sunday morning, while Vivaan was sorting his saved envelopes and e-wallet balances, Amit walked in with his cup of tea.

"You've done pretty well, young man," Amit said, sitting beside him.

Vivaan smiled. "Thanks, Dad. I've saved   ₹8,700! And I haven't even touched the Plan B jar in three months."

Amit nodded thoughtfully. "That's great. But you know what's even better than saving money?"

Vivaan looked up, curious. "What?"

Amit leaned in with a twinkle in his eye. "Earning money from your saved money."

Vivaan said that's already in place Dad, I am earning 3.5% interest on my account.

Amit smiled and told, what if you get almost double.

Vivaan blinked. "You mean... my money can earn even more money?"

Amit laughed. "Exactly. When you keep your money safely in something like a Fixed Deposit—or what we call an FD—the bank actually pays you for keeping it there."

Vivaan's eyes widened. "Wait... the bank gives me money just because I don't spend it?"

"Yup," Amit said. "It's their way of saying thank you for letting them hold your money. The longer you keep it, the more interest you earn."

Vivaan was hooked. "So I can just park my money somewhere and let it grow?"

Amit smiled. "Let me show you."

He took out a small notebook and drew a simple example:

Fixed Deposit Example (1 year)

Amount	₹7,000
Interest Rate	7% per year
Interest Earned	₹490
Total after 1 year	₹7,490

Vivaan stared at the numbers. "I didn't do anything extra and still made ₹490?"

Amit nodded. "That's the power of smart saving, Vivaan. And there are other options too—Recurring Deposits, Mutual Funds, or even learning about how banks work. But FD is the simplest place to begin."

Vivaan sat back, his brain buzzing. "It's like my money is going to school and coming back smarter."

Amit chuckled. "Exactly. And now that Vivaan Enterprises has a decent balance sheet, it's time to make your capital work for you."

Vivaan rubbed his hands together. "Operation: FD begins!"

They spent the rest of the morning going over simple banking terms—principal, interest, maturity date, and how to open a fixed deposit either online or with a form. Vivaan took detailed notes, adding a new section in his ledger titled:

"Vivaan Enterprises – Investment Division"

That night, as he updated his Excel sheet with a column labelled Interest Earned, he whispered to himself, "Next stop—profits without touching the principal. Vivaan Enterprises just levelled up."

Vivaan's eyes sparkled with curiosity. A new idea had taken root in his mind.

What if... I save enough money that the interest I earn every month is enough to cover all my expenses? Then I'd never have to touch my original savings at all!

He leaned back, imagining a future where his money worked for him—quietly earning more while he focused on school, football, and fun.

Could I really live just on interest one day?

The thought felt magical—and very grown-up.

That evening, Vivaan couldn't hold the thought in any longer. As they sat on the balcony, sipping hot chocolate and watching the sunset, he turned to his father.

"Dad," he said, eyes glowing with excitement, "I had this idea... what if I save so much money that I never have to spend my savings at all? Like, if the interest I earn every month is enough to cover everything I need—my food, travel, fun stuff—wouldn't that be awesome?"

Amit looked at Vivaan for a long moment, almost forgetting to sip his tea. There was pride in his eyes, a soft smile tugging at the corner of his lips.

"That's a brilliant thought, Vivaan," he said finally. "It's called living off your passive income. It means your money is working for you, instead of you working for money. A lot of adults aim for that too—it's a part of something called financial independence."

Vivaan grinned. "So it's real? People actually live like that?"

Amit nodded. "Yes, they do. But it takes a lot of planning, patience, and discipline. You're thinking way ahead—and that's incredible."

He paused for a moment, then glanced at Vivaan's eager face, hesitating slightly.

"Though," he added, "there's something else you should know... something people often forget when they plan like this."

"What?" Vivaan asked, leaning in.

Amit scratched his chin. "Well... when the bank gives you interest, or you earn money in other ways without working for it—like from rent, or stocks—that income is still... well, taxable."

Vivaan looked puzzled. "Taxable?"

Amit chuckled gently. "Yes, the government takes a part of that income, like a fee for using public roads, schools, and hospitals—everything we all benefit from. So, if you earn ₹1,000 in interest, you don't actually get to keep the full ₹1,000. You might keep ₹900 or ₹850, depending on the rules."

Vivaan's forehead crinkled. "Oh... so I need to plan for that too?"

Amit nodded. "Exactly. And that's why financial planning is so important. It's not just about earning—it's about understanding where your money goes, how it grows, and what gets deducted."

Vivaan took a long sip of his hot chocolate, deep in thought. "Okay... so Vivaan Enterprises needs to make more than just enough. We need to plan for the taxes too."

Amit smiled proudly. "That's my boy. You're already thinking like a CFO."

They both laughed, and for a moment, the balcony was quiet—just the golden sun, two mugs, and a big dream getting bigger.

A Schoolyard Lesson

During lunch break at school the next day, Aryan peeked over Vivaan's shoulder as he updated his ledger on his tablet.

"What's this new column—interest?" Aryan asked, curious.

Vivaan grinned. "Its money my money earns while doing nothing!"

Aryan blinked. "Like a lazy employee?"

"No, like a smart one!" Vivaan laughed. "It's called a Fixed Deposit. Want me to show you how it works?"

As he explained, a few more classmates gathered around, fascinated. For Vivaan, sharing this knowledge was almost as satisfying as earning the money itself.

Later That Night

After Vivaan had gone to bed—his ledger neatly tucked beside his pillow like a favourite bedtime storybook—Amit sat quietly on the sofa, staring into his cup of tea.

His wife, Neetu, entered the room, wiping her hands on a towel. "You've gone quiet again," she said with a smile, sitting beside him.

Amit sighed, a thoughtful smile on his face. "Vivaan surprised me today... again. He said he wants to earn enough interest from his savings so he never has to touch the principal. Can you imagine? A 12-year-old thinking like that!"

Neetu chuckled, her eyes twinkling. "Our little Vivaan... running a one-man corporation in his mind."

Amit laughed, but then his expression turned serious. "I'm proud of him, Neetu, truly. He understands things most adults struggle with. But sometimes I wonder... am I pushing him too far, too soon? These are heavy concepts—savings, interest, taxes, financial independence. Shouldn't he just be... playing, exploring, and living carefree?"

Neetu placed a gentle hand on his arm. "Amit, you're not forcing anything on him. You're answering the questions he's asking. He's not memorizing charts or doing it to impress you—he genuinely enjoys this."

Amit looked uncertain. "But what if he grows up too fast? Misses the fun of being a child?"

She smiled and leaned back. "Children are like sponges. They absorb more than we think, but they don't always absorb it the way we do. For Vivaan, money isn't stress or pressure—it's curiosity, its play. It's like how some kids build Lego towers, and he builds financial plans. If that's his joy, let him explore it."

Amit considered that for a moment. "You really think he's not losing his childhood in this?"

"No," she said softly. "He's shaping it in his own unique way. And he's lucky—he has a father who doesn't just teach money, but teaches empathy, patience, and balance along with it."

Amit smiled, the weight lifting off his shoulders. "I guess you're right. As long as he's having fun with it... we just keep guiding, not pushing."

Neetu nodded. "Exactly. And if someday he decides to drop all this and start painting or chasing butterflies—we'll support that too."

Amit chuckled. "Fair enough. But until then, I guess I'll be the Chief Mentor of Vivaan Enterprises."

Neetu raised her cup like a toast. "And I'll be the Chairwoman of Emotional Affairs."

They laughed softly, the warmth of their conversation lingering like the aroma of evening chai, while upstairs, Vivaan slept soundly—dreaming, perhaps, of a world where rupee coins turned into golden trees.

9

From Fixed Deposits to Fund Manager Dreams

It was a breezy Sunday afternoon. Vivaan had finished his homework and was sprawled across the floor with his notebook, his "Vivaan Enterprises" ledger open beside him. Amit was lounging on the couch, reading the newspaper, when Vivaan suddenly looked up.

"Dad," he said, "I want to do something smart with the money I've saved."

Amit folded the paper and smiled. "That's the spirit. So, what do you have in mind?"

"I want to invest it," Vivaan said proudly. "Like, make it grow. Can I put it in a fixed deposit?"

Amit raised his eyebrows. "FD? Impressive! Looks like someone's like my suggestions by default."

Vivaan giggled. "I still remember the FD concept you told me earlier. I liked the sound of interest getting added automatically!"

Amit got up, sat beside Vivaan, and pulled the notebook toward him. "Alright then. Let's talk about it seriously."

He drew three simple boxes with arrows and labelled them:

1. Reinvest Principal + Interest
2. Monthly Interest Pay-out
3. Close on Maturity – Deposit to Savings

"These are the three maturity options when you open an FD," he explained. "Let's break them down."

Vivaan leaned in, eyes shining.

Amit pointed to the first. "In the first option, both your savings and the interest it earns are locked in again after maturity or completion of the term —so the amount grows faster over time. It's great if you don't need the money anytime soon."

He moved to the second. "This one gives you monthly interest. You don't grow the savings, but you get a little extra income every month—almost like a pocket money/salary."

"And this last one?" Vivaan asked.

Amit nodded. "At maturity, the full amount goes to your savings account. Good if you want to save now and use it all at once later."

Vivaan tapped his pen thoughtfully. "Okay, okay... let me try calculating the monthly interest one!"

He scribbled quickly:

Principal	₹12,000
Interest Rate	6.5%
Annual Interest	₹780
Monthly	₹65

He looked up. "Only ₹65 a month?"

Amit smiled. "That's right. It's something, but not much. FDs work best when you put in larger amounts. Want to try with more?"

Vivaan nodded eagerly.

Amit thought for a moment, then said, "What if I add ₹2 lakh to your ₹12,000? Let's say we invest ₹ 2,12,000 at 6.5% interest, and we choose the monthly pay-out option. Try that."

Vivaan calculated:

Principal	₹2,12,000
Annual Interest	₹13,780
Monthly	₹1,148.33

"Whoa!" he grinned. "That's over a thousand rupees a month! That's like getting paid every month without doing anything!"

Amit laughed. "Exactly. That's the power of smart saving."

He paused, then added, "But want to hear something even better? There are higher FD rates for senior citizens—like 7.75%. We can book the FD in Grandpa's name."

Vivaan's eyes widened. "Really? That much?"

Amit nodded. "Try calculating it with 7.75%."

Vivaan scribbled:

Principal	2,12,000.00
Interest @7.75% annually	16,430.00
Monthly	1,367.17

"Wow! That's almost ₹1,370 a month!"

Amit gave a proud smile but raised a finger. "Wait—now here's the grown-up part. That amount is taxable. If Grandpa's total income crosses a certain limit, the bank will deduct TDS—Tax Deducted at Source—usually 10%."

Vivaan frowned. "So, 10% of ₹16,430 is... ₹1,643? So actual interest is ₹14,787?"

Amit patted his shoulder. "Correct! So monthly, it'll be around ₹1,232. That's why we always plan after tax."

Vivaan scribbled everything in a new section of his ledger labelled:

FD PLAN – Vivaan Enterprises

He grinned. "Dad, this is awesome! I'm gonna build a Vivaan Bank now!"

Amit chuckled. "Start small, dream big. You've already opened your first branch—in your mind."

10

Slices of Wealth — Vivaan's Mutual Fund Adventure

Over the next few years, Vivaan remained loyal to his pocket money philosophy. But the source had evolved. Instead of eagerly waiting for the 1st of every month, he now waited for his fixed deposit interest. The ₹1,200 or so that arrived monthly became his new pocket money—his personal stipend, not earned through chores or requests, but through mindful saving and patient planning.

He used it wisely. Sometimes for books, sometimes to treat friends to modest snacks, and often to save again. He had unknowingly mastered the art of **delayed gratification**. The question "Do I want it, or do I need it?"—something Amit had once casually asked—had now become his silent mantra.

By the time Vivaan turned sixteen, his transformation was clear. His little ledger had matured into a proper Excel sheet—pie charts, categories, color codes, even graphs. *Vivaan Enterprises* was no longer just a game. It had become a mind-set.

Yet, he remained a typical teenager— Even with all this financial learning, Vivaan lived a **full teenage life**:

- He played as a **wicketkeeper** for his school cricket team and won medals.
- He and his friends would **cycle around the colony**, competing who could ride fastest.
- He **saved from his pocket money** for small dates at cafes, birthday gifts for friends, and festival treats.

He once had to buy a costly cricket bat for team, he convinced team mates to contribute and bought it without hurting anyone's pocket. He also understood the power of mutual funding then.

One day at the school library, flipping through a business magazine, Vivaan's eyes caught a headline:
"How Mutual Funds & Stocks Can Beat Inflation and Earn More"
Curious, he dove in. He read about **compounding returns, equity risks, SIPs (Systematic Investment Plans),** and **index funds**. The idea of "growing wealth faster than FDs" sparked something in him.
That evening, as Amit relaxed with his tea on the balcony, Vivaan slid beside him, a spark in his eye.

"Dad," he asked casually, "you ever invested in mutual funds?"

Amit smiled knowingly. "I was wondering how long it would take you to ask."

Vivaan grinned. "I just read about SIPs. They say it's better than FDs if you want to beat inflation. Is it true?"

Amit nodded. "Yes, but mutual funds aren't as stable. They go up and down. You need patience and discipline. But over time, they can build more wealth."

Vivaan tilted his head thoughtfully. "So… instead of spending my FD interest, what if I start a SIP? Say, ₹1,000 every month?"

Amit raised an eyebrow. "That's a serious thought. You ready to build a portfolio?"

"Why not?" Vivaan smiled. "Vivaan Enterprises is ready to go public!"

Saturday Afternoon – Wealth Meet

Balcony. Lemonade. Almonds.

Amit pulled out a notepad. "Alright. Imagine this…"

He drew a stick figure. "You want a pizza worth ₹1,000. But you only have ₹100."

Vivaan nodded.

"Now imagine 9 friends each bring ₹100. Together, you buy the pizza and share it."

Vivaan smiled. "That's a mutual fund."

"Exactly. A pool of people investing together. The person who decides which pizza to buy is the fund manager."

"Ahh," Vivaan nodded. "So what kinds of pizzas are we talking about?"

Amit laughed. "Types of mutual funds:"

- **Equity Funds** – Risky but with higher potential returns. *Spicy pizza!*
- **Debt Funds** – Stable, low risk. *Plain cheese.*
- **Hybrid Funds** – A mix. *Half and half.*

"And how do I earn from them?" Vivaan asked.

"When the value of that pizza—your investment—goes up, your slice becomes more valuable. That's your return."

Vivaan leaned back. "So it's like group work in school, but with money."

"Exactly," said Amit. "Except if the pizza gets burnt, everyone's share drops. That's the risk."

Vivaan's next question came naturally:

"How do I choose the right fund?"

Amit scribbled three big questions on the paper:

1. **What is your goal?**
   (Are you just hungry for now? Or saving appetite for a big party later?)

2. **How much risk can you handle?**
   (Do you like experimenting with spicy pizzas, or prefer simple cheese that's always safe?)
3. **How much time can you wait?**
   (Do you want a quick snack, or are you willing to wait and enjoy a grand feast?)

Vivaan chuckled. "So, if I want quick returns, I go for a different fund, and if I want to build big money over 10 years, I choose another?"

"Exactly!" said Amit. "Short-term goals need safer funds, like debt or hybrid funds. Long-term goals can go for equity funds, where you stay invested and ride the ups and downs."

Vivaan thought for a moment. "And how do I start? Do I need to go to a bank?"

Amit shook his head. "No, son. These days, it's all online. There are apps and websites where you can choose and invest easily. You just need a PAN card, a bank account, and KYC—Know Your Customer details."

Vivaan's face fell a little. "PAN card? I don't have one yet."

Amit smiled warmly. "Don't worry. You're just starting to learn. For now, we can do it in my name, but we'll create a small 'Vivaan Enterprises Portfolio.' You'll be the brain behind it."

Vivaan's eyes lit up again.

Amit continued, "We'll start with a mock investment first. We'll create a sample portfolio, track it for a few months, and then when you turn 18, you'll be ready to invest your own money, properly and legally."

Vivaan nodded seriously. "Deal. But Dad, can I choose the funds?"

"Of course. With a little guidance. Remember, Vivaan Enterprises doesn't invest blindly!" Amit said, ruffling his hair.

The Mock Portfolio – Vivaan Enterprises Trial Run

That evening they sat together, exploring mutual fund categories:

- Large-cap funds
- Mid-cap funds
- Index funds
- Balanced advantage funds

Amit explained each like different pizza toppings—some safe, some adventurous, and some a surprise mix.
That night, Vivaan fell asleep dreaming not of cricket or video games, but of building wealth, one slice at a time.
Amit said, "Okay boss, now pick three funds for your trial portfolio. One from each category: Safe, Moderate, and Adventurous."
Vivaan thought for a while and made his choices:

- **Safe**: A **Large-Cap Fund** that invests in big, strong companies.
- **Moderate**: A **Balanced Advantage Fund** — part stocks, part bonds, changing according to market conditions.
- **Adventurous**: A **Mid-Cap Fund** with slightly smaller companies that can grow faster but are also riskier.

Amit handed him a task:
"Pick three funds: Safe, Moderate, and Adventurous."
Vivaan chose:

Fund Type (Risk)	Reason for Choosing
Large Cap (Low)	Fund – X - Stability of strong companies
Balanced Advantage (Medium)	Fund – Y - Balanced mix
Mid Cap (High)	Fund –Z - Growth potential

They pretended to invest   ₹500 in each and tracked them month by month.

The Rollercoaster Begins

At first, Vivaan checked his sheet every day.
    One day: +1.5% in the mid-cap fund. He jumped with joy.
Two days later: -2%. He panicked.
    "Dad! Should I sell everything?"
    Amit laughed. "Vivaan, relax. Don't judge a cricket match in the first 5 overs."
    Vivaan smiled. He got the message.

Three Months Later

After tracking patiently (with some ups and downs), Vivaan saw that:

- His Large Cap fund grew slowly but steadily.
- His Balanced Fund moved less, staying mostly flat.
- His Mid Cap fund jumped up and down like a rollercoaster — but overall gained the most!

The final "mock returns" over three months were:

Fund	Average return after 3 months
Large Cap Fund	+3%
Balanced Advantage Fund	+2%
Mid Cap Fund	+7%

Vivaan was ecstatic. His fixed deposit was generating interest, and he was channelling that income directly into his SIP investments — all without lifting a finger. The idea of earning returns on his returns filled him with excitement.

More importantly, he was learning to handle market mood swings without fear.

Amit was proud. "You've done well, son. And you know what? Most adults don't even have this much patience."

Vivaan puffed up with pride and thought to himself:

"*Vivaan Enterprises* is not just about saving anymore. It's about building."

Over the Next Two Years…

Vivaan continued learning, but didn't lose balance. He juggled:

- **School projects**
- **Cricket tournaments**
- **Hangouts with friends**
- **Wealth Meets with Amit** (One Saturday every month)

Amit had one rule:

"Finance should be part of your life—not your whole life."

Key Learnings:

SIP = Buying pizza slice by slice

Equity Funds = Growth

Debt Funds = Safety

Hybrid = Balance

Concepts like CAGR, Expense Ratio, and Goal-Based Investing

Goal Tracker with:

- Short-Term: New cricket kit
- Medium-Term: Laptop for college
- Long-Term: ₹5 lakh portfolio by age 22

Vivaan's journey was no longer just about saving money. It had become about building wealth with wisdom.

A penny saved is a penny earned!

11

CEO at 18 — The Handover

As Vivaan's 18th birthday approached, he wasn't just counting candles — he was counting milestones.

Over the past few years, he had grown steadily—not just in height or confidence, but in wisdom. He now had:

- A solid understanding of **risk and return**
- Clarity on **investment types** and their behaviours
- The **discipline** to track and review his finances
- And above all — **the patience** to let time work its magic

He had learned one of life's most important lessons early on: *Money isn't everything, but knowing how to use it well can shape everything.*

18th Birthday – A New Chapter for Vivaan Enterprises

It was a bright, cheerful Sunday morning. The house buzzed with laughter, colourful balloons danced in the breeze, and the sweet aroma of chocolate cake filled the air. Friends and family had gathered to celebrate a major milestone — Vivaan turning 18.

He received thoughtful gifts — books he'd wanted, new cricket gear, clothes, even a digital planner. But there was one gift, wrapped in the simplest form, that caught his attention immediately: a plain white envelope with just three words on it — **"To the CEO"** — written in Amit's familiar handwriting.

As the party wound down and the sun dipped gently into the horizon, Amit called Vivaan into the study. Just the two of them.

No cake. No noise. Just a quiet moment that felt monumental.

Amit handed Vivaan the envelope and said with a smile full of pride,

"This is the final official act of the Founder of Vivaan Enterprises."

Vivaan smiled and opened it slowly, already sensing its weight. Inside was a handwritten letter — neat, heartfelt, and overflowing with emotion.

The Letter

Dear CEO Vivaan,

Congratulations! Today, you step into adulthood — not just legally, but financially, emotionally, and mentally. You are now the sole decision-maker and custodian of your life's most important enterprise — *your future.*

Enclosed in this envelope are:

- Your **mutual fund folio numbers**
- Updated **bank account details**
- **SIP mandates** to be transferred in your name
- And a **roadmap** you helped design with intention and clarity

For years, you've shown how to save, invest, enjoy, reflect, and bounce back from mistakes.
You've lived the true spirit of **Vivaan Enterprises**.

From today, I step aside as Founder and hand over full control to you — the CEO.

Build it. Protect it. Grow it.
But above all — *enjoy it.*

With love, trust, and immense pride,

Your first investor and biggest fan,
Dad

Vivaan stared at the letter, a lump rising in his throat. He had thought he was prepared. He had rehearsed this handover in his mind countless times. But the emotions hit different when the moment was real.

He hugged Amit tightly.

"Thank you, Dad... not just for this, but for believing in me right from the start."

Amit smiled, patting his back gently.

"You're ready, son. You've built a strong foundation. Now, go dream bigger. Remember — Vivaan Enterprises doesn't just manage money. It manages happiness."

Vivaan nodded, wiping a quiet tear from his cheek.

He took a deep breath and looked out the window.

The sun had set — but a new light was rising inside him.

"This is just the beginning."

You've taken the first step by reading this book. Now, take your learning into the real world. Talk about money with your parents/kids, start tracking your spending, save consistently, and keep investing in your knowledge. Remember, every rupee has a purpose—your job is to find it.

www.ingramcontent.com/pod-product-compliance
Lightning Source LLC
Chambersburg PA
CBHW040151110726
48005CB00018B/2728